TIFFANY HADDISH

TIFFANY
HADDISH

KEVIN HALL

Rosen
YA™

New York

Published in 2020 by The Rosen Publishing Group, Inc.
29 East 21st Street, New York, NY 10010

First Edition

Library of Congress Cataloging-in-Publication Data

Names: Hall, Kevin, 1990– author.
Title: Tiffany Haddish / Kevin Hall.
Description: First edition. | New York : Rosen Publishing, 2020. | Series: The giants of comedy | Includes bibliographical references and index.
Identifiers: LCCN 2018052175 | ISBN 9781508188612 (library bound) | ISBN 9781508188605 (paperback)
Subjects: LCSH: Haddish, Tiffany, 1979-—Juvenile literature. | African American women comedians—Biography. | African American actors—Biography.
Classification: LCC PN2287.H165 H35 2020 | DDC 792.7/6028092 [B]—dc23
LC record available at https://lccn.loc.gov/2018052175

Manufactured in China

On the cover: Tiffany Haddish burst into the entertainment mainstream in 2017; she is shown here at the 2017 NAACP Image Awards.

CONTENTS

Introduction

She is one of Hollywood's most popular stars. She has been in various movies, television shows, and commercials. She is also a rising star in the world of traditional stand-up comedy. Tiffany Haddish has become an undeniable force in the entertainment industry since storming into the mainstream in 2017 with *Girls Trip*. She has an infectious energy and spirit, and she elevates every project in which she stars. How did she rise to such fame? Tiffany Haddish's story is an intriguing and inspiring one. Through great adversity, and with determination and hard work, she has risen to great heights in the entertainment world today.

Historically, the world of comedy has been dominated by white men, whether they played leading characters in blockbuster comedy films or stood alone onstage performing stand-up. Black comedians—male or female—were often relegated to bit characters or secondary roles, rarely used to

Tiffany Haddish is one of today's most popular entertainers. Her rise to fame—through adversity and countless challenges—is an inspiring tale.

appeal to a mainstream audience. Following in the footsteps of superstar Kevin Hart, however, Tiffany Haddish has broken through racial and gender barriers to become a household name all across the United States. She has leveraged her success in blockbuster movies into a burgeoning career in music, stand-up, and more. Haddish's rise to fame is an inspiring story that demonstrates how far people are willing to go to reach their dreams and the hard work required to achieve lofty goals.

CHAPTER ONE

Humble Beginnings

Tiffany Haddish was born in Los Angeles, California, on December 3, 1979, to parents Tsihaye and Leola Haddish. Tsihaye, Tiffany's birth father, left the family when she was three years old, and her mother went on to remarry and have more children. Tiffany would soon become the oldest of five siblings. However, she would soon become much, much more than that.

Troubles in Childhood

In 1988, when Tiffany was nine years old, her stepfather tampered with the brakes on Leola's car. His original intention was to harm Leola as well as her five children, but Tiffany and the rest of her siblings chose to stay home the day Leola crashed her car due to the tampering. Leola suffered significant brain damage due to this accident. This brain damage may have led to Leola's eventual diagnosis of schizophrenia, which made it extremely hard for her to take care of the family. Tiffany, at that point still very young, was forced to become the primary caregiver for the family. "I was basically a 10-year-old mom. I was feeding [my siblings] and dressing them. I was taking care of everybody," she told Patrick Gomez of *People*. This, sadly, included her mother: "Everything my mom had taught me for the first nine years of my life, now I was teaching her."

Tiffany tried—day in and day out—to be the mother Leola could no longer be by doing things like paying bills and making sure her siblings got to school. However, it proved to be too much for her. Three years later, she and her siblings were placed in foster care. Tiffany was separated from her siblings, and despite efforts to remain in touch with them, she found it increasingly difficult to reach out to them. This was yet another blow to young Tiffany. Not only did she lose her mother but she also lost the only family she had ever known.

When Haddish was fifteen, she was fortunate enough to be reunited with her siblings. The pain of losing them subsided, and her life, although still far from stable, looked familiar again. However, there were struggles. Though she can hardly be blamed given her erratic and unsettled life at home, Haddish started acting up at school. Her current career as a comedian had its origins here, as she used humor as an escape and a way to make sense of the world around her.

Being funny was how Haddish dealt with the new families she lived with in foster care and the separation of her real family, including her mother. Being the class clown at school was a great remedy for her personal life, but it also proved to be a disruption. She used comedy as a distraction from her studies. Despite this, her teenage years were some of the first times Tiffany realized she could use comedy as a way to protect herself from the negative parts of her life.

USING COMEDY AS A CURE

Tiffany Haddish is not the only comedian who has used pain as fuel for comedy. Countless other comedians have struggled in their lives. Instead of feeling sorry for themselves, many comedians will be inspired by their own pain, using jokes as a way to ease their struggles while also making audiences laugh. This does not mean every single comedian has had a tragic past. Those who have suffered

(continued on the next page)

(continued from the previous page)

Kevin Hart is one of many comedians who have used the pain in their lives as fuel for their stand-up careers. He and Haddish are good friends.

hardships, however, often have a unique perspective in their jokes. There is an old saying that claims that comedy is "tragedy plus time." Haddish and other comedians have put this saying to use.

One example of a comedian with a difficult past is Kevin Hart (also a friend of Haddish). In many of his comedy routines—particularly those early in his career—Hart discusses the challenges he faced growing up, including (like Haddish) having an absentee father. Audiences have responded well to his humorous takes on the adversity of his life, as they have also done with Haddish.

Too Much Clown, Not Enough Class

After entering high school, Haddish found herself drawn to various entertainment outlets. She became El Camino Real High School's mascot, performing in costume for her classmates. She bested several hundred other contestants to win a prize for delivering Shakespearean monologues and started working as a DJ at local bar mitzvahs as a way to earn money. She learned how to use her vibrant and outgoing personality to her advantage, laying the foundation for her later career.

Haddish attended El Camino Real High School in Los Angeles. It was there that she first realized her love of entertaining, performing, and making people laugh.

However, as Haddish's attraction to humor got stronger, her behavior in school continued to get worse. Though she was involved in several extracurricular activities, she was finding it difficult to maintain focus in the classroom. As her priorities shifted from academics to comedy, she found an unexpected benefit: if she could make her classmates laugh, sometimes they would let her copy their homework. This allowed her to get by, but she was not learning the material on her own, which

The Laugh Factory provided Haddish an outlet with its comedy camp. Her time there would prove very valuable for her.

meant she continued to struggle when she could not copy someone else's work.

Concerned over her poor behavior, her social worker—who had been assigned to Haddish's case since she had been in foster care—gave her one final chance to redeem herself: she could either spend time with a psychiatrist or attend camp at the Laugh Factory, a well-known comedy club in Los Angeles. Unsurprisingly, she chose the latter.

THE LAUGH FACTORY SAVES THE DAY

The Laugh Factory Comedy Camp has been operating since 1984. The club's owner, Jamie Masada, reaches out to underprivileged children in the Los Angeles community every year and provides around thirty of them the chance to attend an eight-week stand-up comedy camp. The camp is free for all those who are selected. Each attendee is evaluated based off his or her desire to perform stand-up in the future. Each student is encouraged to use his or her anger, frustrations, and hurts and channel those feelings into comedy. The campers are coached by professional comedians. Some comedians who have volunteered for the program in the past include Adam Sandler, Dave Chappelle, Chris Rock, Dane Cook, and Jim Carrey.

Tiffany Haddish is not the only person who attended the camp who went on to have a successful career in entertainment. Some others include Nick Cannon and Amanda Bynes. The camp itself was included in a 2002 PBS documentary *Stand Up: A Summer at Comedy Camp* that aired nationwide. Masada and the staff at the Laugh Factory have provided a valuable service for the community for decades. It provides a unique environment for at-risk youth to prosper and discover their talents. It worked for Haddish, and there is no telling how many other stars will find their voices through the program.

Life-Changing Laughs

Haddish's experiences at the Laugh Factory Comedy Camp in 1994 would help define the rest of her life. She received encouragement and advice from famous comedians including Richard Pryor, the Wayans Brothers, Dane Cook, and many other big-name comic stars. It was during her experiences at the Laugh Factory that Haddish first realized she had a passion for comedy. Instead of using it just to coast by in school and navigate her life's challenges, she realized she could use her past experiences in her act. The stage soon became a safe haven for her. She used her pain as comedy fuel, and her dream of becoming a stand-up comedian took hold as she progressed at the comedy camp.

Haddish had the privilege of being surrounded by comedy superstars during her time at the Laugh Factory Comedy Camp, but there was one person

The Wayans Brothers became two of the many mentors for Tiffany as she progressed onstage and as a person during the Laugh Factory Comedy Camp.

in particular who stood out: Charles Fleischer. Fleischer is a comedian best known for voicing Roger Rabbit from the classic comedy *Who Framed Roger Rabbit?* Haddish recalls that the film was a defining work in her life.

Haddish explained to Liz Shannon Miller of IndieWire.com that there is a pivotal scene in the movie that helped her realize her potential. Detective Eddie asks Roger Rabbit why all the other characters are doing such nice things for him. Roger responds with "because I make 'em laugh, Eddie. If you make people laugh they'll do anything for you." That is where it clicked for Haddish. She realized she could become successful by making people laugh. While it may seem like an unlikely source, *Who Framed Roger Rabbit?* served as one of Haddish's main sources of inspiration during her long journey in comedy.

Charles Fleischer was one of Haddish's earliest inspirations in comedy. Meeting him in the early part of her stand-up career helped motivate her to keep going.

Meeting the voice of Roger Rabbit during the comedy camp only cemented her desire to pursue comedy. Comedy was not just a coping mechanism for her anymore—it was what she was meant to do. Fleischer's Roger Rabbit was just one of many influences on Haddish's life. Although she did not find success immediately after attending the comedy camp, she took the positivity of her role models to heart.

Another key figure Haddish met at the Laugh Factory was comedy legend Richard Pryor. During one of her sets, Pryor interrupted her, telling Tiffany she was not telling a joke at all. He told her that comedy audiences are going to comedy shows because they want to have fun. They are not interested in being reminded about the horrible things going on in the world or a person's own problems. He advised Haddish to focus more on having fun onstage—if she enjoys herself, the audience will, too. She took that advice to heart. No matter if she was in class goofing off or onstage working out a new joke, it all came back to Pryor's advice: just have fun.

Haddish made such an impression on her coaches and fellow campers that a local news channel ran a story about her journey into comedy. The publicity from this story allowed her to keep performing, and she transitioned from

Richard Pryor is one of the true legends of the comedy world. Like Haddish, he also used painful parts of his life as fuel for his material—but he knew how to have fun with it.

doing sets during the day to appearing on shows at night and on weekends, when the crowds were much bigger. However, this was short-lived. At the age of eighteen, she decided to quit stand-up in order to make a more steady, consistent living. She would eventually find herself back onstage years later, but after completing high school, Haddish found herself working a variety of odd jobs trying to survive.

The Struggle Continues

Though she made a lot of inroads during her time at the Laugh Factory, Haddish's personal life continued to be a challenge. In her memoir, *The Last Black Unicorn*, she opened up about an experience she endured when she was seventeen years old. On the night of her homecoming dance, she was raped by a police cadet. Though she reported the sexual assault, she has not confirmed that justice was served to her attacker.

This experience had a direct impact on Haddish, especially when dealing with directors and producers during auditions in show business. Audiences today know Haddish as a vibrant, energetic, and unapologetically loud performer. Though she has always been outgoing and not afraid to speak up, surviving her sexual assault caused her to emphasize those traits. The horrifying experience taught her not to back down, and to stand up for herself aggressively. Haddish did not allow this horrible event—or any other hardship—to define her. She continued to push forward, even as life tried to drag her down.

The years following Haddish's high school graduation were full of dead-end jobs, volatile relationships, and many other difficulties that were similar to her troubled times in childhood and as a teenager. In *The Last Black Unicorn*, Haddish described a relationship she had with a man named Titus, whom she met in 2001. She and Titus dated for about eight months without any real problems. Then, Titus met a pimp, and everything changed.

Titus started asking Haddish whether he should become a pimp himself, and their relationship rapidly deteriorated. The couple drifted apart, spending less and less time with one another. Haddish then announced to Titus's family that she would be going on a cruise. Titus managed to also find his way on the cruise as well.

On the trip, he hounded Haddish, following her and criticizing her for talking to different men. To make matters worse, the cruise happened the week of the September 11 terrorist attacks in New

York City. With the airports shut down, Haddish paid extra money to stay on the boat for four days. Then, after getting home from the extended cruise and finding evidence that Titus was cheating on her, Haddish ended their relationship. However, things in her personal life were about to get much, much worse. Titus's behavior on the cruise was part of a much larger saga in Haddish's young life.

CHAPTER TWO

The Ex-Husband

Titus was not the only person on Haddish's mind when she went on that extended cruise in 2001. On the plane ride, she met and started talking to a police officer named William Stewart. She believed it would be nice to have a black friend who was a police officer, so she and Stewart made an immediate connection. They found out that they were going on the same cruise.

Part of the reason Titus was so enraged with Haddish during the cruise was because Stewart kept following Haddish around the ship and filming her. Because of his constant presence, Titus became jealous and accused Haddish of sneaking out and cheating on him with Stewart. Despite having no romantic relationship with Stewart, she was still confronted by Titus repeatedly about her involvement with this other man.

In the early 2000s, Haddish had difficulty balancing her blossoming stand-up career with her relationships.

Much like Titus himself, Stewart followed Haddish everywhere she went on the ship, filming her the entire time and continuing to provoke Titus. Because Haddish had no intention of continuing a relationship with Titus after the cruise, she exchanged phone numbers with Stewart, hoping to reconnect with him. Then, nothing happened for five years.

Five Years Later

After half a decade of no communication, Stewart reached out to Haddish. After watching her appearance on *Bill Bellamy's Who's Got Jokes?*—a stand-up comedy television show— Stewart found her new contact information through someone else. After reconnecting, Stewart did not waste any time with his intentions: he said he wanted to marry Haddish. Though this seems like

Bill Bellamy provided Haddish with an opportunity to grow her career by appearing on his show. It was an important milestone for her, and it helped her influence grow.

a strange pronouncement after five years without any communication, he told her that watching his videos of her from the cruise always gave him a smile. He also promised Haddish that he would find her birth father, whom she had not seen for many years, if she agreed to see him. In hindsight,

Stewart's obsession with creating a romantic relationship with Haddish and his admission that he watched videos of her frequently should have been warning signs. However, at the time, she found these behaviors endearing.

After so many failed relationships, Haddish believed that this phone call was a sign. She was hoping a man would come along who would truly care about her, and although Stewart's call came out of nowhere, she believed deep down that it was an answer to her prayers and that she should strike up a relationship. She truly believed that this was the man she was looking for. The fact that the man waited five years to reach out to her—in addition to his other strange actions—was not a cause for concern for her.

Things became even more serious when, three weeks after Stewart's initial phone call, Haddish's birth father called her. She now had a difficult decision to make. Could she really go through with this and seek a long-term relationship with someone who was essentially a stranger? Engaging in any relationship was difficult enough for her, and starting a relationship with someone she barely knew would be a challenging obstacle to overcome.

She and Stewart continued talking after he located her father. Then, she booked a movie filming in New Orleans, Louisiana, and let Stewart know she would be out of town. Thinking nothing of it, she left to go shoot the film. Without warning, Stewart showed up. Haddish had only let him know that she was shooting a movie in New Orleans—she did not reveal the name, the exact location, or any other specific details that would tip off where she would actually be. Nonetheless, this man was determined to see her.

THE SIGNS OF A STALKER

Though Haddish did not notice it early on, Stewart was showing signs that he was a stalker. Many of his actions fit the profile of someone obsessed with another person. These included:

- Filming someone without his or her permission and watching that film later
- Following someone who is not a friend or family member around, with or without that person's knowledge
- Making uninvited and unexpected attempts to contact someone
- Finding someone's contact information through a third party

A stalker, though he or she may seem harmless—or affectionate—at first, can quickly put the person being stalked in a dangerous situation. No healthy relationship is based on this behavior.

- Attempting to immediately start a serious relationship, such as by proposing marriage, without knowing the other person well
- Showing up unannounced and uninvited to someone's home or workplace

Though there are many other ways a person can exhibit signs of being a stalker, these are among the most common—and Stewart checked every box. Haddish did not recognize the dangers of these behaviors, but anyone who feels someone is stalking him or her should contact local law enforcement immediately.

More Warning Signs

Haddish was surprised, though not alarmed, by Stewart's sudden appearance in New Orleans. She knew that he drove from Atlanta, Georgia, to meet up with her, and she knew that he must have found out her exact location from someone else. Haddish did not react negatively to these behaviors, but Stewart's obsession was forming a pattern.

However, he was nothing but polite to Haddish in New Orleans. He did not make any awkward advances, and he even tidied up her trailer as she was shooting the movie. Although his history of unusual behavior should have put Haddish on alert, his actions after he made it to New Orleans made it seem like the man genuinely cared about her.

Although his visit was not lengthy, Stewart and Haddish had made an impact on each other. She called him the following weekend while drunk, and the very next day, he drove out again to see her. It was during this visit that she began to feel real affection for Stewart. Sure, the man took five years to even get in touch with her again, but it seemed as though he cared about her, and he seemed to be the answer to her wishes to have a decent man in her life. He was willing to drive hours and hours at the drop of a hat to see her. He was clearly unlike the rest of the men Haddish had dealt with in her life, but the question remained: Was she really ready to have a full-blown relationship with someone she barely knew?

The Birth of a Relationship

The weekend after Stewart's second trip to New Orleans was his birthday. Instead of paying Haddish another visit, he offered to buy her a plane ticket to visit him in Atlanta. This was just another example of how he was beginning to win her over. He had bought her gifts and treated her well when he came to New Orleans. He had located her birth father. Now, he was flying her out to see him. Despite the red flags that should have been raised at many of his actions, Haddish believed Stewart was different from the other men in her life, and it made her think that she may not encounter anyone like him ever again. In *The Last Black Unicorn*, Haddish admits that she was not particularly attracted to his appearance, but his generosity and kindness had impressed her, and she felt he deserved a chance at a relationship.

After they had spent time together in Atlanta, Haddish wasted no time in reminding Stewart that he had offered to marry her. He had not forgotten, and after driving to Virginia in order to meet her birth father, Stewart made plans to propose to her in public at a comedy club. After the proposal and

Despite her troubles with Stewart, Haddish's move to Los Angeles in the mid-2000s helped boost her comedy career; she is shown here attending Comedy Central's Emmy after-party.

eventual marriage in 2006, the two headed out to Los Angeles to start their lives together. It was in California, however, that everything began to unravel.

In another impressive gesture, Stewart gave Haddish a new car. She initially thought that this was just another example of the man's generosity, a testament to how much he truly cared about her. However, she later found out a disturbing truth about this so-called gift: Stewart had planted a tracking device on the car. He wanted to keep track of Haddish always, monitoring where she was going at all times of the day. She also remembered being followed by one of Stewart's friends. While Haddish still did not recognize that Stewart had an unhealthy obsession with her, his actions were shifting, from simply creepy and somewhat inappropriate to ugly and potentially dangerous.

More Surprises

As Stewart's actions became more sinister and controlling, Haddish found out about another part of his life: he had an existing family. He told her he had three kids, and he brought his eight-year-old son with him when he moved to California to be with her. They lived in Haddish's one-bedroom apartment for a month, and then he purchased a new, bigger home. However, the home was located more than an hour away from Los Angeles. Stewart relocated them out of town on purpose: he wanted Haddish all to himself, and he tried isolating her from her friends as well as her dreams of continuing to pursue comedy as a career. However, Haddish continued performing, which did not at all please Stewart. He told her that she did not need to keep doing comedy, as he was making good money. This was one of the first times he tried to exert direct control over Haddish's life. He tried to get her away from comedy—the one thing that managed to keep her sane and stable throughout her life. He wanted to be in complete control, but Haddish defied him, and kept pursuing her passion.

THE SIGNS OF A CONTROLLING RELATIONSHIP

Haddish's marriage had all the textbook signs of a controlling relationship. Because she had never had a positive romantic relationship before, though, she struggled to recognize the danger she was in.

A controlling relationship can take an emotional—and sometimes physical—toll on the people involved. Though it can be difficult, as it was for Haddish, the person being controlled should defend himself or herself from being controlled.

Eventually, however, she realized that Stewart wanted her all for himself and was willing to go to great lengths in order to make sure this happened. Some signs of an inappropriately controlling relationship are:

- Tracking where a partner goes
- Aggressively telling a partner what to do
- Threatening a partner, either emotionally or physically
- Intentionally isolating a partner from family and friends
- Controlling a partner's career decisions

(continued on the next page)

(continued from the previous page)

Many times, a controlling relationship exists because one person wants his or her partner to act a certain way. In a healthy relationship, both partners can talk about their expectations and, if they disagree, they break up. In an unhealthy relationship, one person can become controlling and try to force his or her partner to conform to his or her desires. Any person who feels he or she is being inappropriately controlled should talk to his or her partner and, if necessary, end that relationship.

After his attempts to directly control Haddish failed, Stewart told her she was expected to act as the mother for his eight-year old son. She was instructed to attend school meetings, drop him off at sports, and perform other parental duties. This was a form of indirectly trying to control Haddish—after all, if she were busy taking care of a child, she would not have time to pursue her career goals.

For Haddish, being in charge of a child was something that she was not expecting, but it was something she was used to. Considering the mental state of her own mother growing up, she was certainly accustomed to taking on the mother role in a family. However, the circumstances this time were much, much different. Haddish was not performing at clubs and casinos every night when she was raising her own family. This time, she was juggling the care of a young child, a husband who was trying to control her every move, and her blossoming acting and stand-up comedy career. Stewart even tried controlling her content, demanding that she not talk about his son in any of her material. This was yet another example on the growing list of controlling actions he was taking. He was trying to dominate every facet of Haddish's life—but she was not going to follow his directions.

Unfortunate Escalation

Unfortunately, many controlling relationships— like the one between Haddish and Stewart—end poorly, with a large fight and a bitter breakup. In other cases, they end in violence, and this was the case for Haddish. In *The Last Black Unicorn*, she recalls Stewart choking her. She fought back, but the violence continued despite her best efforts. She tried moving back to her old apartment to get away from him, but she ended up taking him back after a short break.

This was another moment of unfortunate judgment for Haddish, but it is a common occurence in controlling, abusive relationships.

Often, an abuser convinces his or her victim that the abuse is not as bad as he or she thinks, or the abuser convinces his or her victim to blame himself or herself. Despite Stewart's behavior being suspicious, controlling, and violent, he was such a pivotal part of her world at the time that they ended up back together. It was easy enough to say that she was going to leave him—but actually doing it was much harder.

After they got back together, Stewart's controlling behavior continued—but so did Haddish's rise in the world of stand-up comedy. In 2010, she was invited to perform at Montreal's Just for Laughs Festival in Canada. Just for Laughs is one of the most prominent comedy festivals in the world, and many famous comedians and actors use the festival as a chance to showcase their talents and book gigs in sitcoms and movies. This was a golden opportunity for Haddish to advance her career.

She was scheduled to perform at the festival and stay in Montreal for two weeks. During the second week, Stewart unexpectedly showed up to be there with her. His behavior there was unfortunately similar to his behavior on the cruise: he never left Haddish's side. Again, she did not realize this was another example of his controlling, obsessive behavior; she accepted that this was part of his personality and, consequently, part of their relationship.

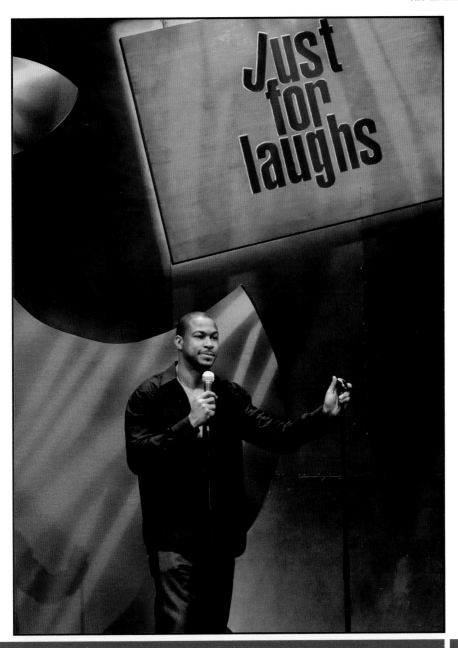

The Just for Laughs festival is a gathering place for comedy's top stars. Finesse Mitchell is one of the many stars who have performed at the Just for Laughs festival over the years.

Stewart's behavior only became more erratic as he spent more time in Montreal. He began accosting other famous comedians, and then, unfortunately, he abused Haddish once again. The comedians, audiences, comedy executives, and everyone else at the festival could clearly see that she was suffering in this relationship. However, she found she could not simply leave him and walk away from their marriage.

Leaving Problems

In *The Last Black Unicorn*, Haddish admitted that one of the prime reasons for her not leaving Stewart was that this relationship was one of the first huge commitments she had made in her life. She did not want to be seen as a quitter, and despite all of the wrongdoing and trouble he had put her through, she wanted to see things through. She truly thought that she could find a way out of this, and she did not want to give up. She thought that Stewart was the only man who really loved her. This kind of rationalizing is unfortunately common among many victims of domestic abuse. Despite the obvious red flags, the people telling her to get out, and the likelihood that things would not get any better, Haddish stuck by him.

After the Just for Laughs incident, Stewart gave his wife a set of rules. These included when she could go out and see people and when she could send and receive text messages. These rules— already an offensive form of partner abuse—began having an effect on her stand-up career. Haddish had to decline stand-up gigs because they would interfere with the new rules he set for her. Despite her commitment to stay, she realized things would just stay the same or get even worse.

Things finally came to a head when Haddish realized Stewart was speaking to other women. This was what finally broke her. After more physical abuse—including an incident in 2011 during which the police were called and Haddish filed for a restraining order against Stewart—Haddish finally moved on. Her entire relationship with Stewart was one of the most challenging, confusing, and awful times of her life. She has occasionally brought up this terrible relationship in her stand-up act, but it is a difficult subject for her to discuss.

Even after all of Stewart's attempts to manipulate, control, and smother Haddish's comedy career, she persevered. Throughout the saga of abuse and reconciliation that plagued that time in her life, she was performing in clubs, acting, and making a name for herself in comedy circles. By the time she finally broke things off with Stewart—for good—she was ready to make a big entrance in show business.

CHAPTER
THREE

Still Rising

Tiffany Haddish's road to success in comedy was a long, painstaking one. Many comedians have to work on their craft for years and years before they finally hit it big, and she was no exception. After her divorce from Stewart—and as she began diving back into the world of comedy—she did shows all throughout Los Angeles. She would travel up to two hours for shows, and she continued making money by working as an entertainer at bar mitzvahs. Working these events took her all across the country, and she was making more money with those events than when she was performing stand-up throughout California. However, she knew deep down that her real passion was stand-up, and she continued getting onstage and honing her act, night after night.

Even before seeking a divorce from Stewart, Haddish was hard at work, building her reputation in California and staking a claim as an up-and-coming black comedy star.

Breaking Through, Breaking Down

Before her rocky relationship with Stewart, one pivotal moment in Haddish's career was appearing on the show *Bill Bellamy's Who's Got Jokes?* in 2006. Hosted by esteemed comedian Bill Bellamy, *Who's Got Jokes?* pits four comedians against each other. Each performer must perform three minutes of clean comedy. If a performer goes over his or her time or uses profanity, that comedian is docked points. Haddish managed to win the first round of competition, and she was slated to then continue performing. However, in the later rounds, she was forced to perform in Atlanta—instead of in California, where she had honed her act for so many years.

In the second round of competition, she performed for more than 3,000 people, and she completely botched the timing of one of her opening jokes. In frustration after hearing criticism from the audience, she reacted by swearing. In a regular comedy setting, this would be seen as slightly unprofessional but not a huge deal. However, because this was on live television, it was seen as a colossal failure. Haddish not only bombed during her set but she was also dismissed from *Who's*

Got Jokes? An opportunity that could have helped launch her career was all but wasted, and she felt as if her comedic life was doomed. People were seeking out the clip, and she feared it would scare off any potential gigs. Fortunately for her, she would have plenty more opportunities to make her mark on the stand-up world.

Even though she tanked during the second round of competition, getting to the second stage at all on *Who's Got Jokes?* helped Haddish land other roles and gigs. She made it onto HBO's *Def Comedy Jam*, which led to even more opportunities for her. In 2009, she had a bit part in the Mike Epps and Ice Cube movie *Janky Promoters.* The film was only released to a small audience, yet it proved that the debacle on *Who's Got Jokes?* would not derail Haddish's career. *Janky Promoters* also helped her start booking gigs at colleges.

Collegiate Comedy

The opportunity to perform at colleges throughout the United States was yet another landmark achievement in Haddish's blossoming comedy career. Many famous comedians start out on the college circuit, making thousands of dollars per performance. However, in the 2010s, many entertainers have spoken out against performing at colleges at all.

Haddish is shown here performing with her trademark energy, enthusiasm, and outrageous personality on HBO's *Def Comedy Jam* in 2007.

Chris Rock and Jerry Seinfeld have both admitted that they do not enjoy performing at schools. This is because of the current age of political correctness, which they claim has taken over college campuses. Many colleges will discuss what material is forbidden from shows on campus. Jokes about race, sexuality, and other sensitive subjects may be disallowed. Not every college has the same guidelines, and comedians like Haddish often sign contracts before they perform, agreeing upon what can and cannot be said onstage.

During this time, Haddish remembered the advice comedy legend Richard Pryor gave to her all those years ago during the Laugh Factory Comedy Camp: just have fun. A touring comedian has to enjoy himself or herself, no matter if he or she is performing in sold-out college auditoriums or for an almost-empty bar. Haddish, who was performing night in and night out, learned to have fun as she interacted with different audiences and learned how to develop her material into longer, funnier sets.

During the early 2010s, Haddish had several shows that demonstrated both the glorious ups and depressing lows of a touring stand-up comedian. During one performance, the heel on one of her shoes broke. Unfazed and with

Chris Rock is one of the many prominent comedians who have spoken out against the difficulties that go along with performing at many colleges in the twenty-first century.

razor-sharp wit, she took that misfortune and riffed on it for ten minutes to amazing comedic effect, winning over the audience and adding even more jokes to her act.

One of her worst sets was during a college show at Howard University. Haddish was an opening act for the famous comedian Tony Rock, and there were thousands of students in attendance. Her material did not win over the crowd at all, and her jokes were met with silence instead of laughter. Her set was so poorly received that after she was done, her manager called and said she would only be paid a portion of what she had been promised. Though Haddish would have had legal justification to ask for the full amount she was promised, the entertainment industry does not look kindly on inexperienced performers who speak out. She did not fight for the money she was owed—the money she rightfully earned—because doing so would have been risking her future career goals.

Learning the Ins and Outs

By the time Haddish was making waves on the college performance circuit, she was establishing herself as an energetic, entertaining comic. However, the nature of stand-up comedy was one she was still trying to truly navigate. As a black woman performing in an industry primarily dominated by white men, she faced a lot of unique—and difficult— challenges. Though she was breaking more and more into the mainstream, appearing in movies and on television, she was still often regarded as a second-rate comedian. In *The Last Black Unicorn*, she described several occurrences of male comics trying to take advantage of her, trying to devalue her comedy, and refusing to regard her with the respect she had earned.

THE MYTH OF WOMEN NOT BEING FUNNY

Because so many successful comedians throughout history have been men, some people believe that women simply are not capable of being funny. There are many contributing factors to this idea. In the early days of modern comedy, most successful comedians were men, and men had more access to opportunities to appear both onstage as well as in movies than women did. Just as in many industries, comedy became known as a man's field, unwelcoming to women.

(continued on the next page)

(continued from the previous page)

Wanda Sykes is one of the many women who have established careers in comedy. There are countless successful female comedians who prove women are just as funny as men.

In the 2000s, however, the tide started to change. Now, female comedians (or comediennes) have many more open opportunities for breaking into the mainstream. Tiffany Haddish—among countless other women—is an example that completely disproves the idea that women cannot be funny. There are dozens of superstar female comedians and entertainers, including Wanda Sykes, Roseanne Barr, Ellen Degeneres, and Kate McKinnon. All of these women have put in just as much time, effort, and passion as their male counterparts—and it shows.

Making her reputation as a comic in Los Angeles was a huge step for Haddish, and she kept rising and earning new lucrative opportunities. However, the stigma of being a female performer followed her everywhere she went. She battled bookers and talent agents who told her the only way she could get onstage was to provide sexual favors, instead relying on her talent. Strong-willed and defiant, she refused to give in to these inappropriate demands, and her hard work proved that she could be a success in the comedy world by focusing on her act—not by breaking down and giving in to the harassment and sexist behavior around her. After all, the most important thing for a comedian—of any gender—is to be funny. If Haddish had given in to the demands of shady agents, she would have been selling herself short. Instead, she persevered and kept climbing the comedy ladder.

A Big (Little) Friend

From a young age, Haddish had been fortunate enough to have many interactions and friendships with famous actors and comedians. At the Laugh Factory Comedy Camp, during the birth of her performing career, she was introduced to some of the biggest names in the comedy world. However, there was one friendship in particular that elevated Haddish and helped keep her going. It was with a comedian who, like her, worked for years to become both a prominent stand-up comedian as well as a tour de force in the acting world: Kevin Hart.

Kevin Hart is one of the best-known comedians in the world today. However, as Haddish was struggling to make it as a comedian, he also became a source of guidance and inspiration for her. Hart noticed her talent immediately and encouraged her to keep going at it and to not give up, despite her hardships. At the time Hart and Haddish first interacted, she was at one of her lowest points. She was living in her car since she could not afford rent.

This is where Hart came into play. Not only did he offer encouragement for Haddish to keep

Kevin Hart was one of the many figures who helped Haddish as she established herself as a force in the comedy world. Both comedians have become household names across the United States and around the world.

pursuing her dreams but he also helped her with her living situation. Sympathizing with her struggles, he gave her $300 so she could find a hotel room to sleep in—a temporary escape from homelessness. Beyond that, Hart made her focus on her own career and what she wanted, both out of life and with her comedy. He told her to write down a list of goals she wanted to achieve, as a reminder of where she is and where she wants to be.

Haddish's number-one wish then was for an apartment, and thanks to Hart's connections in California, he was able to find her one almost immediately. Despite the fact that it was in a less-than-desirable neighborhood, she was grateful for what he provided. An apartment in a bad neighborhood is still much better than living in a car. Haddish, who had had such awful experiences with men and others in the entertainment industry prior to this, remained grateful to Hart as they both progressed in their respective careers.

This burgeoning friendship was a unique experience for her. With her turbulent childhood, relationship woes, and incidents on the stand-up circuit, she was used to being treated poorly. She had grown accustomed to feeling like she did not exist or matter at all. Hart's simple act of kindness made her realize that not everyone was out to get her. Not every man was the same. They were not all terrible, trying to manipulate and control every single aspect of her life. Just by providing her with some money and a place to stay, Hart showed Haddish that men could be positive influences in her life. This simple act of kindness would have long-lasting consequences, as their friendship continued to blossom along with their careers.

The Big Breakthrough

Through all her hardships and years of performing, Haddish experienced mild success. She was fairly well known around Los Angeles—and she was cast in several small roles in small-to-medium films—but she had not yet broken into the mainstream. For many performers, all it takes to be launched into superstardom is a single breakthrough performance. Haddish would get her chance in the summer of 2017 with the movie *Girls Trip*.

Girls Trip was released in theaters on July 21, 2017. The film stars Jada Pinkett Smith, Regina King, Queen Latifah, and Tiffany Haddish as "the Flossy Posse," a group of lifelong friends who have grown apart over the years. When lifestyle guru Ryan (King) is offered to be a keynote speaker at a music festival in New Orleans, she uses this work vacation as a way to reunite her friends. The movie details the ups and downs the four friends have over the weekend in New Orleans.

In *Girls Trip*—which featured a star-studded main cast, shown here—Haddish proved that she was ready to take center stage as an entertainer.

Queen Latifah plays Sasha, a former journalist who owns and operates a struggling gossip site. Jada Pinkett Smith plays Lisa, an uptight single mother. Haddish plays Dina, an energetic, life-of-the-party character. Despite the overwhelming star power in the cast, it does not take long for Haddish to steal the show.

At the beginning of *Girls Trip*, Haddish's character is let go from her job for physically assaulting a coworker. She flat out refuses to accept her termination and acts as if everything is normal and her job will be there for her when she returns from New Orleans. Her behavior becomes wild as the Flossy Posse are on their flight to New Orleans. Dina orders multiple alcoholic drinks, despite the flight being less than an hour. Haddish is a fireball of energy throughout *Girls Trip*, and these two scenes are just two of the many examples that illustrate this. She brings her undeniable energy and infectious enthusiasm to the role.

Haddish's effortless mastery of aggressive physical comedy is once again demonstrated in a later scene. Ryan's business partner and husband—Stuart—is also attending the music festival. Sasha is sent a picture of Stuart with another woman. When she shares this photo with Dina and Lisa, they are reluctant to tell Ryan. However, when they do reveal the secret, Ryan tells them she already knows about the situation and the two are in counseling to try and fix the problems in their relationship. Despite this, things do not go well for Stuart when Dina encounters him in a hotel. She smashes a bottle and threatens her friend's partner in yet another memorable scene.

Haddish is captivating in every scene she has in *Girls Trip*, and the critical reviews of the film all include the fact that Haddish had truly announced herself to the world in her breakout role as Dina. Further success followed.

The True Impact of *Girls Trip*

Girls Trip was an undeniable triumph, earning more than $100 million at the box office. Additionally, it was not just a vehicle for Haddish to show off her amazing comedic abilities to the world. The film was also produced, written, and directed by black filmmakers. It was the first movie to predominantly star black actors and feature black production managers to make $100 million and was the only comedy—overall—to do so during 2017.

The impact of *Girls Trip* goes far beyond how much money it made at the box office. Any comedy—a genre that typically features low budgets and low profits—that makes $100 million is going to attract some attention. However, a comedy that makes that much during the summer makes the film all the more intriguing. Thousands of movies are released each year. There is somewhat of a pattern behind when exactly these films appear in theaters. Movies that premiere closer to the end of the year are typically contenders for Academy Awards. They highlight either a superb ensemble cast or a particular actor or actress who delivers a tremendous performance. On the other hand, movies that are not expected to do well are commonly released earlier in the year. This has become somewhat of a dead period for the movie business, where movies that are not expected to earn a lot of money or garner any awards are cast aside.

One period where many movies are released and expected to do well is during the summer. Many blockbuster films are released during the summer, and one prime example is most superhero movies. Superhero movies are often box office gold because they attract audiences of all shapes and sizes, and they have themes (the battle between good and evil, for example) that are universally appealing. These movies tend to make upward of $1 billion, and they stay in theaters for most of the summer months and are sometimes viewed multiple times by the same audiences.

Girls Trip was released in the month of July, right in the middle of the summer blockbuster season. It stayed at the top of the box office for multiple weeks and earned the producers a tidy profit. For any movie to earn so much during this time—let alone a comedy with a primarily black cast—is truly remarkable. Though it is a hugely entertaining movie, *Girls Trip* does not feature the same themes and elements as most summer blockbusters. For one, many summer

The success of *Girls Trip*, which competed with various blockbuster films, was a milestone achievement. It is one of the most successful films to ever feature a primarily black cast.

blockbusters are a continuation of a beloved franchise. For example, the Marvel Cinematic Universe tends to release a film featuring a specific, well-known superhero every summer. These are announced months (and sometimes even years) in advance to build up hype for the film.

On the other hand, *Girls Trip* was not a continuation of any preexisting story—but Haddish, Queen Latifah, Pinkett Smith, and King were superheroes in their own right. They combined forces to help carry a movie that did not receive the same treatment as other summer blockbusters.

Perhaps the greatest impact *Girls Trip* had on the world of comedy is the explosion of Haddish's career. As a star in a movie with high profits, she immediately got more attention from Hollywood producers and other big names in show business. Her fiery blend of funny and fierce got her global attention, and she has continued her career climb from there, using *Girls Trip* as a launching point.

CHAPTER FOUR

Other Successes and the Future

Although the success of *Girls Trip* helped launch Haddish's career, it was a moment prior to the filming of the movie when she realized she had truly succeeded in Hollywood. It was a pivotal moment for the comedy superstar, as it opened doors for her for films and other projects: she appeared on *The Arsenio Hall Show*. It was with this appearance that she believed she had arrived and was going to be a huge celebrity in show business. Arsenio Hall was one of her idols growing up, and one of her childhood goals was to make it on his show. Unfortunately for her, the original version of *The Arsenio Hall Show* went off the air in 1994. For much of her early career, it appeared that she would never be able to achieve this dream.

Arsenio Hall's original show, which ran from 1989 to 1994, featured many big-name guests, such as Bill Clinton. Hall himself became an idol for many viewers, including Haddish.

Tiffany and *The Arsenio Hall Show*

Fortunately, however, *The Arsenio Hall Show* was revived nineteen years later in 2013. Haddish—who was building her reputation around this time—finally had a chance to meet her idol. When the show originally aired, she was only making classmates and teachers laugh. Now, almost two decades later, she was establishing herself as a full-on comedy powerhouse. She was ready.

A friend of Haddish's was booked to appear on the show, and she seized this chance to ask if she could make an appearance of any kind. She appeared in a sketch the first time. The producers of the retooled *Arsenio Hall Show* enjoyed her and asked her to come back for a second taping. Then they asked her to come back for a third time. During each taping, she asked if she could perform her stand-up act on the show. The producers finally relented in 2014 and she was allowed to appear on the show; this was her big moment.

Arsenio Hall introduced her to the stage by saying she was funny, beautiful, and smart. Hearing these compliments from her childhood idol was overwhelming for Haddish. She had a great set on the show, but what most people remember is what happened after. Hall congratulated her, and then cradled her in his arms like a baby. The crowd went wild. Then, somehow, it got weirder.

Haddish was not exaggerating when she said Hall was her idol. After achieving the lifelong dream of appearing on his show, she did not know how to react. In her trademark off-the-wall comedic genius, she started licking Hall's face. Including that original performance, she would wind up appearing on the modern version of *The Arsenio Hall Show* seven times. She even became a correspondent, interacting with the audience. Unfortunately, not

Haddish and Hall worked together several times on his rebooted show. These appearances were yet another chance for her to demonstrate her comedy skills in the big leagues.

long after all these appearances, the rebooted *Arsenio Hall Show* was canceled.

However, just because Haddish lost her dream platform to do stand-up (and lick people's faces), that did not mean her career would be lost as well. There were many people behind the scenes that she connected with who helped further her career. Tyler Perry, famous for his series of *Madea* films as well as various other television projects, was there to see her perform. He invited her to audition for one of his shows. From that audition, Tiffany was able to land roles on *Girls Trip* as well as *The Carmichael Show*, which both were acclaimed by audiences worldwide. Though it may seem odd that a public appearance that involved licking the host's face led to such incredible opportunities, it is not at all surprising. Haddish's life has been so chaotic, so full of the highest of highs and the lowest of lows that, in a way, it makes sense that these opportunities would fall into her lap.

The Carmichael Show

After her stint on *The Arsenio Hall Show*, Haddish remained on the television circuit, performing on different shows. One of these television shows was the hit *The Carmichael Show*. *The Carmichael Show* stars comedian and actor Jerrod Carmichael as a fictionalized version of himself living in Charlotte,

The Carmichael Show was a launching pad for Haddish and costars Lil Rel Howery, Jerrod Carmichael, and many other comics who appeared on the program.

North Carolina. Carmichael is joined by Haddish, "Lil Rel" Howery, Loretta Devine, and David Alan Grier.

Haddish portrays Nekeisha Williams-Carmichael, who is the ex-wife (and eventual roommate) of Howery's character, Bobby. The show was another vehicle for her blossoming talent. Additionally, the show was also noteworthy for tackling taboo topics many television sitcoms do not try to address. Episodes have been dedicated to issues such as transgender people, the fallout from Bill Cosby's sexual assault trial, the morning-after pill, and various other topics many shows avoid.

The cast of *The Carmichael Show* had nothing but good things to say about Haddish during her time there. Carmichael said she was a natural performer, one who clearly benefited from being around such comedy giants as David Alan Grier and Loretta Devine. Additionally, her role on the show helped her land a spot in the film *Keanu*, which undoubtedly caught the eyes of the people behind *Girls Trip.*

Keanu came out in theaters in April 2016. The film stars comedy duo Keegan-Michael Key and Jordan Peele, known for their work on *MadTV* as well as their hit Comedy Central show *Key & Peele.* The two star as best friends who must infiltrate a vicious gang in order to save a kitten the gang took from them. The premise is deliberately absurd, and Key and Peele's sometimes-strange comedic style was a natural fit for Haddish.

Although *Keanu* was intended to showcase the talents of Key and Peele, Haddish also makes her mark in the film. She stars as Trina "Hi-C" Parker, an undercover police officer who, like her costars, pretends to be part of the gang scene to take down the main villains in charge.

It was very hard to miss Haddish following her roles in *The Carmichael Show*, *Keanu*, and *Girls Trip*. She appeared in the 2018 basketball comedy *Uncle Drew* alongside basketball superstars Kyrie Irving, Shaquille O'Neal, Reggie Miller, Chris Webber, and many others. She went from blowing an opportunity

Haddish (*center*) teamed up with esteemed comedy duo Keegan-Michael Key (*back, second from right*) and Jordan Peele (*front right*) for their successful first attempt at filmmaking: the comedy hit *Keanu.*

on live television to acting with some of the basketball world's most famous stars. This career turnaround is just another example of her tireless work ethic and how far she has come in her years acting and performing stand-up.

One effect filming *Girls Trip* had on Haddish was the relationship she forged with her costars. Not only are Haddish, Queen Latifah, Regina King, and Jada Pinkett Smith friends in the movie but they also became very friendly in real life. This tends to happen a lot in Hollywood. Filming can be a grueling process, and when a group of people spends that much time together, they often forge powerful personal connections.

The Fourth of J. Blige

The bonds of friendship from *Girls Trip* were so strong that Queen Latifah invited Haddish to her house for a Fourth of July party in 2017. Haddish brought along some friends, including esteemed comedian Hannibal Buress and *Carmichael Show* costar Howery. Despite being a celebrity herself, Haddish still had a tendency to get flustered and act a little starstruck around other celebrities (one example of this being Arsenio Hall).

As the party progressed, Haddish recognized another major celebrity: famous singer Mary J. Blige. Not afraid to introduce herself, Haddish went over and said how much she loved her music. At this point, she had been at the party for a long time and had been drinking. As she started cracking jokes with Blige, the singer offered her more drinks. Queen Latifah soon intervened and told Haddish to get back inside, however, before she drunkenly did something to embarrass herself. The next day, on the set of *Girls Trip*,

Meeting and becoming friends with legendary singer Mary J. Blige was one of many examples of Haddish's charisma and likable personality.

Queen Latifah and Jada Pinkett Smith made fun of her antics during the party.

However, instead of alienating herself from Blige, Haddish's actions had the opposite effect. Just as her incident with Hall actually produced a positive reaction, the same was true with her interaction with Blige. A representative for the singer contacted Haddish weeks after the party to request that the two spend more time together. They explained that Blige was going through a rough divorce, and she needed someone like Haddish to be there for her to cheer her up when she needed it.

After making connections in Hollywood and becoming a household name across the United States, Haddish's career was really taking off. Another film she starred in following the success of *Girls Trip* and *Keanu* was 2018's *The Oath*. Haddish stars alongside veteran comedian Ike Barinholtz as the wife in an interracial couple. The film takes place in a future where all American citizens are required by law to sign "The Patriot's Oath," a legal document that must be submitted to the US president by Black Friday. The film details a raucous Thanksgiving dinner that soon descends into chaos. Critics praised both Barinholtz and Haddish in their roles in the film.

THE COLLISION OF COMEDY AND POLITICS

The release of *The Oath* in 2018 can be interpreted as a reaction to the political atmosphere in America. Since the election of President Donald Trump in 2016, there have been countless movies, television shows, and other creations that have addressed the political divide in America that has persisted throughout the country since (and prior to) the election in 2016.

The Oath is a relatable movie in that it takes place over one of the more volatile weekends for many families across the United States: Thanksgiving weekend. Family members with differing political opinions can argue on social media or ignore each other entirely, and the Thanksgiving holiday becomes a battlefield for many families. *The Oath*, along with various other films and shows, illustrates this point.

More broadly, politics and comedy have been connected for a long time. Comedy media is so important to Americans that politicians have made cameo appearances in various comedy films and shows. Trump himself hosted *Saturday Night Live* prior to his election. The relationship between politics and comedy goes far beyond this most

(continued on the next page)

(continued from the previous page)

recent election, as comedians and actors have been parodying famous political figures for decades. (Kate McKinnon has famously portrayed Trump's opponent in 2016, Hillary Clinton, on *Saturday Night Live*.) Because of the enormous political divide in the 2010s, though, comedy and politics have interacted more and more, and Haddish's role in *The Oath* is an extension of that interaction.

Award-Show Haddish

For much of Haddish's long career in Hollywood, her main accomplishments were countless memorable performances as well as box office reports. However, she had yet to bring home any awards. This all changed in late 2017. In November 2017, she was the host on *Saturday Night Live*. The show, entering its fourth decade, remains one of the most popular comedy shows on television, with superstar guests and quick-witted sketches. Hosting the show was just another milestone in Haddish's already illustrious entertainment career. This time, however, people were really paying attention—and they were ready to reward her for her efforts.

Haddish responded to her 2018 Emmy in predictable fashion: with a quick-witted joke. This was the first of many major achievements in her burgeoning career.

In 2018, Haddish won the Emmy for Best Guest Actress in a Comedy Series for hosting *Saturday Night Live*. However, when asked if she felt proud for taking home an Emmy, her response was a little unusual. She said she was not as proud of the Emmy because it did not come with any cash payment. She had assumed people were so obsessed with awards like Oscars and Emmys because they were accompanied with some form of prize money, so she was jokingly disappointed to receive only the award and a gift bag.

The Concern with Cash

It may seem selfish of Haddish to say that she was not all that impressed with winning an Emmy. However, there is something noble about how concerned she is about the money she makes from her stand-up and acting gigs. Though many entertainers are heavily invested in winning awards, they rarely discuss the money involved in show business. Haddish is different. Because she did not come from wealth or have formal training at a prestigious institution, she is very aware of the hardships of the performance industry. After all, even though she is able to follow her passion, it is still her job to be funny, and she needs to be paid. She is concerned about keeping a roof over her head and being able to provide for her family.

Haddish recognizes the importance of winning awards—like her Emmy—but she also understands that a trophy cannot keep her from going back to living in her car.

Her interest in compensation also ties in to how she approaches a very polarizing topic in Hollywood: the difference in pay between actors and actresses. Haddish is a firm believer in asking for the "guy fee" for every project in which she is involved, she revealed to Debra Birnbaum of *Variety*. This means she negotiates her salary based on how much a male performer would make for a similar role. This is a brilliant method to use. She obviously knows how much she is worth and is not going to let her gender impact her earnings.

This issue extends far beyond Hollywood. The pay gap is an issue that has permeated nearly every industry, in the United States and around the world. Unfortunately, women in various professions sometimes find themselves making far less money than their male counterparts. In many ways, Haddish serves as a role model for any woman who feels she should be earning more money. She is not afraid to demand what she feels she is worth for a television show or film project. In an industry where many people are obsessed with how they are perceived and the awards they think they deserve, Haddish is more concerned that her acting and stand-up gigs

In a full-circle moment, Haddish starred alongside comic and longtime friend Kevin Hart in 2018's *Night School*, in which she plays an aggressive but caring teacher.

support her and those around her. She brings her famously fearless and fierce personality to all her negotiations, and she is not afraid to stand up for herself—and for all women.

In the time since her career skyrocketed with *Keanu*, *Girls Trip*, and various other projects, Haddish has not shied away from the spotlight. Rather, she has completely embraced it. She has gone on to star in several movies, including *Night School*, *Uncle Drew*, and *Nobody's Fool* in 2018 alone.

Coming Full Circle

Tiffany Haddish and Kevin Hart—who have known each other before either became the sensation he or she is today—now find themselves some of the most in-demand comics in Hollywood. In another major career milestone, she starred alongside Hart in the film *Night School,* released in September 2018. She stars as a high school teacher who attempts to teach Hart so he can earn his GED. This is a full-circle performance for Haddish not only because of the history she has with Hart but also because of the film's subject matter itself.

Hollywood allows its stars to enter completely new worlds, and *Night School*, though not as successful a hit as *Girls Trip*, serves as an important benchmark for Haddish. Growing up, she often struggled in school, and her behavior in high school caused further challenges. However, with her role as an instructor in *Night School*, she is conquering some parts of her old life. She is a competent teacher in the film, which speaks to her drive and determination, especially in the wake of her own struggles growing up. Though *Night School* was not as well received as some of Haddish's other films, sharing the screen with her longtime friend was a big moment.

What the Future Holds

If 2017 was the year Tiffany Haddish broke into the mainstream, the years after have been a continuation of her success. She has a lot on her plate, playing a major role in the sitcom *The Last O.G.* The show stars Tracy Morgan as Tray, an ex-convict who returns to his native Brooklyn after serving fifteen years in prison. Haddish plays Shay, Tray's ex-girlfriend. The show instantly became a smash hit and was another accomplishment for the comedy superstar.

With a number of successful sitcoms and hit movies under her belt, it is easy to see why Haddish is regarded as one of the world's prominent comedic voices. Going along with her rising fame have been increased opportunities. Alongside comedian Ali Wong, she is voicing one of the main characters in the Netflix series *Tuca and Bertie*. She is also lending her voice talents to *The Lego Movie 2: The Second Part*, playing Queen Watevra Wa-Nabi. She also has a starring role in the films *Nobody's Fool* and *The Kitchen*. Starting with the breakout *Girls Trip*, Haddish is doing everything she can to cement her legacy as a Hollywood comedy legend, and her work ethic—influenced by her turbulent childhood— has elevated her status in show business.

Tiffany Haddish's story is an inspiring one, and one that almost did not happen at all. Had she been in the car with her mother during that tragic accident, there is no telling if she would have made it to Hollywood and become the superstar she is today.

When *Girls Trip* launched Haddish into the Hollywood mainstream, there were signs Haddish would grow into the comedy superstar she is today. In

Through a challenging childhood, rocky relationships, and comedy miscues, Tiffany Haddish has risen to be an elite entertainer—and her fans cannot wait to see what she does next.

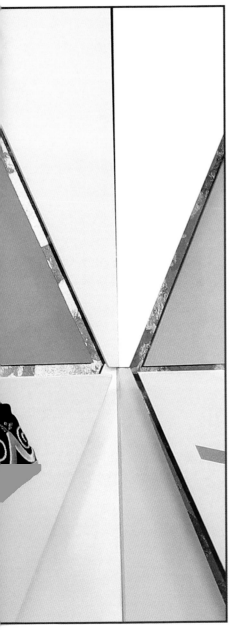

her review for the *Chicago Tribune*, Katie Walsh wrote, "This is Haddish's movie, and will make her a star. It's clear from the moment she hits the screen." Haddish has had the tools around her from the start. The various comedians at the Laugh Factory Comedy Camp served as her very first tutors, encouraging her to take the pain in her life and translate it into bits for her stand-up act. She had fellow comedians— including Kevin Hart, "Lil Rel" Howery, and Arsenio Hall—to uplift her and encourage her to keep going. She used stand-up as a way to escape, to make the pain of her life bearable. Without comedy, Haddish's life would have been completely different. Using her skills as a comedian, she has been able to take ownership of her hardships instead of surrendering to them.

Tiffany Haddish has become an entertainment icon. She is a raucous, irreverent, sometimes filthy comedian and actress who illuminates the screen (or stage) every time she appears. She is unforgettable, leaving her mark on everything in which she is involved. There is no stopping her and also no telling what she will do next. Her hero, the animated Roger Rabbit, once said that "if you can make them laugh, they'll do anything for you." Tiffany has followed this advice. She continues to make people laugh, and they will continue to pay attention as she blossoms into the superstar she was destined to become.

Fact Sheet on Tiffany Haddish

Full name: Tiffany Sarac Haddish
Birthplace: South Los Angeles, California
Birthdate: December 3, 1979
Parents: Leola Haddish and Tsihaye Reda Haddish
High school: El Camino Real High School
Favorite television shows: *It's Always Sunny in Philadelphia*, *@midnight*, *Def Comedy Jam*
Height: 5 feet 6 inches (167 cm)
Comedic influences: Roger Fleischer, Richard Pryor, Arsenio Hall
Career when she wasn't a comedian: Bar mitzvah entertainer
Funniest person she knows: Kevin Hart

Fact Sheet <small>on Tiffany Haddish's Work</small>

Comedy Specials
2017 *Tiffany Haddish: She Ready! From the Hood to Hollywood*

Television Credits
2005 *That's So Raven*, "When in Dome," Charlotte
2006 *My Name Is Earl*, "The Bounty Hunter," Robin
2006 *Bill Bellamy's Who's Got Jokes?*, "Warm It Up in LA," herself
2007 *Just Jordan*, "Krumpshakers," Diamond
2009 *Secret Girlfriend*, "You and Your Ex Call It Quits," Jessica's coworker
2013–2014 *Real Husbands of Hollywood*, multiple episodes, Tiffany
2014 *New Girl*, "Exes," Leslie
2014–2015 *If Loving You Is Wrong*, multiple episodes, Jackie
2015–2017 *The Carmichael Show*, multiple episodes, Nekeisha
2016–2017 *Legends of Chamberlain Heights*, multiple episodes, Cindy (voice)
2017 *Saturday Night Live*, "Tiffany Haddish/Taylor Swift," host
2018–2019 *The Last O.G.*, multiple episodes, Shay
2019 *Tuca & Bertie*, multiple episodes, Tuca (voice)

Film Credits

2008 *Meet the Spartans*, Urban Girl
2009 *Janky Promoters*, Michelle
2012 *Boosters*, Debra
2014 *School Dance*, Trina
2016 *Keanu*, Trina "Hi-C" Parker
2017 *Mad Families*, Keko
2017 *Girls Trip*, Dina
2018 *Uncle Drew*, Jess
2018 *The Oath*, Kai
2018 *Night School*, Carrie
2018 *Nobody's Fool*, Tanya
2019 *The Lego Movie 2: The Second Part*, Queen Watevra Wa-Nabi (voice)
2019 *The Secret Life of Pets 2*, Sonya (voice)
2019 *The Kitchen*, Ruby O'Carroll

Video Game Credits

2009 *Terminator Salvation*—Equity Games, Resistance Soldier (voice)

Music Video Appearances

2017 "Moonlight," by Jay-Z
2018 "Nice for What," by Drake

Books

2017 *The Last Black Unicorn*, published by Simon & Schuster

Critical Reviews

Girls Trip

"There's plenty of star power behind *Girls Trip*, including always-bankable director Malcolm D. Lee and big names like Queen Latifah and Jada Pinkett Smith, but the film's biggest breakout belongs to relative newcomer Tiffany Haddish, who makes off with not only the comedy's best lines and bits of physical humor, but its most eye-popping performance. Best known to mainstream audiences for her work on *Keanu* and *The Carmichael Show*, Haddish has been working steadily since 2005, but *Girls Trip* seems destined to launch her into the big time (it doesn't hurt that she's also got her first stand-up special teed up for an August debut on Showtime). And it should, because she's the best thing going in a film that has plenty else to recommend it, especially for audiences eager to see a truly wild summer comedy." —Kate Erbland, IndieWire.com

"Haddish is a genius technician of physical comedy, at once subtle and gigantic. Watching her hunt down a man, clutching a broken champagne bottle, you almost expect her to go through with slashing him. She lurches, bumps, and grinds; she curls her lips, twists her neck, wags her wide tongue … Her most memorable lines have the surging rhythm of ad lib."—Doreen St. Félix, *New Yorker*

The Oath

"Not only is she a consummate master of comedy
on par with Madeline Kahn and Carole Lombard,
she inherited their knack for being equally adept
at evoking the blistering, chaotic winds of a
hurricane and its peaceful eye. This is not to say
that Haddish cannot handle something more
dramatic—in *The Oath* she has a very effective
crying scene. But she is at her best when her
characters are dropped into escalating situations
that require them to forcefully react."—Odie
Henderson, RogerEbert.com

Comedy

"I think the best thing about Tiffany is seeing her rise.
Also, remembering when I was in that same place
and how excited I was when all the opportunities
kept coming. Watching the same thing happen
for her and even bigger is so dope to see. She's
enjoying it, she's humbled by it. She's appreciative
of the moments."—Kevin Hart, *Atlanta Black Star*

Timeline

1979 Haddish is born on December 3 in Los Angeles, California.

1982 Haddish's father leaves the family. Her mother remarries and has more children.

1988 Tiffany's stepfather tampers with the brakes on her mother's car. Her mother suffers serious brain damage, forcing Tiffany to take control of the family.

1991 Haddish and her siblings are separated in foster care.

1994 Haddish and her siblings are reunited under the care of her grandmother.

1997 Haddish graduates from El Camino Real High School. She attends the Laugh Factory Comedy Camp, meeting legends Richard Pryor, Dane Cook, and Charles Fleischer.

1999–2009 Haddish struggles to make it in stand-up and works in various jobs, including customer service at Alaska Airlines. She lives in her car for a short time.

2013 Haddish lands a recurring role on *Real Husbands of Hollywood*.

2014 Haddish lands the role of Nekeisha on *The Carmichael Show*.

2016 Haddish costars with Jordan Peele and Keegan-Michael Key in the film *Keanu*.

2017 In what became her breakout role, Haddish costars alongside Jada Pinkett Smith, Regina

Hall, and Queen Latifah in the smash hit *Girls Trip*. She releases a stand-up special, *Tiffany Haddish: She Ready! From the Hood to Hollywood*. She hosts *Saturday Night Live* and is the first female black stand-up comic to do so.

2018 Haddish wins an Emmy Award for her hosting role on *Saturday Night Live*. She stars in the films *Night School, Nobody's Fool,* and *The Oath*.

Glossary

audience The people who view or witness a performance.

bar mitzvah A religious ceremony for a Jewish boy who, when he turns thirteen, is officially a man.

blockbuster A movie expected to perform well at the box office and earn awards.

bombing In stand-up comedy, when a performer has an unusually bad performance that can hurt his or her chances of landing more gigs or acting roles.

booking The act of arranging a stand-up or acting performance.

box office The place where tickets are sold to the public for admission to an event; also refers generally to total ticket sales for a film.

cast The collection of actors and actresses that star in a production.

circuit A series of venues for performances on a tour.

clean comedy Comedy that is appropriate for all ages and avoids profanity and explicit topics.

comedy festival A gathering of comedians who perform multiple shows over several days in the same location.

cruise A vacation trip on a boat that usually stops at several destinations.

dirty comedy Comedy that is full of vulgarity and adult topics.

divorce The act of terminating a marriage.

DJ Short for disc jockey; a person who selects and plays music at an event.

documentary A type of film that provides a factual report on a real-life topic.

domestic abuse Acts of violence committed by one partner in a relationship against the other.

erratic Seemingly random, out of control, or difficult to predict.

fiancée A woman engaged to be married.

foster care A system in which children are placed into group homes approved by the state.

gigs Scheduled performances for an entertainer.

hype Excitement or anticipation for something, such as a movie.

inroads Connections and contacts within a certain industry.

material A comedian's jokes and ideas for shows.

obsessive The state of being totally fixated upon someone or something.

opening act A comic who performs a shorter set before the main headlining or featured comedians.

pimp Someone who illegally controls sex workers and profits from them.

political correctness Language and measures used to avoid marginalizing a certain group of people.

profanity The use of swears and other inappropriate language and conduct.

red flag A warning sign that indicates trouble.

schizophrenia A mental health issue characterized by the inability to feel, think, or behave normally.

sexist Describing actions that discriminate based on a person's sex.

shoot To record a film or television show.

social worker Someone who helps those in poor living conditions.

stalker Someone who harasses another person with obsessive, uninvited, and unwanted attention.

stand-up comedy A style of comedy where a performer tells jokes stories in front of a live audience.

For More Information

Black Ensemble Theater
4450 N. Clark Street
Chicago, IL
(773) 769-4451
Website: https://blackensembletheater.org
Facebook: @BlackEnsembleTheater
Twitter and Instagram: @blackensemble
This theater organization provides black actors,
   singers, and other entertainers the chance to
   audition and find new roles.

The Comedy Store
8433 Sunset Boulevard
Los Angeles, CA
(323) 650-6268
Website: https://thecomedystore.com
Facebook, Twitter, and Instagram: @TheComedyStore
Along with The Laugh Factory, The Comedy Store is
   a great destination for comedy in Los Angeles.
   Many comics, including Tiffany Haddish, have
   graced the stage over the years.

Just for Laughs
2095 Laurent Boulevard
Montreal, QC H2X 2T5
Canada
(514) 845-2322
Website: https://www.hahaha.com/en

Facebook, Twitter, and Instagram: @justforlaughs
The Just for Laughs Festival is one of the most
popular comedy festivals in the world. It features
up-and-coming comedians, established
veterans, and multiple showcases over a long,
fun weekend.

Ladies of Comedy Association (LOCA)
Website: https://www.theladiesofcomedy.com
Twitter: @ladiesofcomedy
Based in both Los Angeles and New York City, this
bicoastal organization is dedicated to helping
women in comedy succeed.

The Laugh Factory
8001 Sunset Boulevard
Los Angeles, CA 90046
Website: http://www.laughfactory.com
Facebook: @LaughFactoryHollywood
Twitter: @TheLaughFactory
Instagram: @laughfactoryhw
The Laugh Factory is one of Los Angeles's most
famous clubs in the United States.

National Comedy Center
203 West Second Street
Jamestown, NY 14701
(716) 484-2222
Website: http://www.comedycenter.org

Facebook: @nationalcomedycenter

Twitter and Instagram: @NtlComedyCenter

This new museum is a great asset for those who love comedy. It has various exhibits on the history of comedy, comedy legends, and much, much more.

For Further Reading

Allen, T. L. *Achievements & Legacies of Famous African Americans: Black Entertainers*. n.p.: CreateSpace, 2015.

Brown, Austin Channing. *I'm Still Here: Black Dignity in a World Made for Whiteness*. New York, NY: Convergent Books, 2018.

Durbin, Karen. *The Allure of Beauty: Women in Hollywood*. New York, NY: Assouline, 2008.

Fain, Kimberly. *Black Hollywood: From Butlers to Superheroes, the Changing Role of African American Men in the Movies*. Santa Barbara, CA: Praeger, 2015.

Fauset, Jessie Redmon. *Comedy: American Style*. Mineola, NY: Dover Publications, 2013.

Fearn-Banks, Kathleen, and Anne Burford-Johnson. *Historical Dictionary of African American Television*. Lanham, MD: Rowman & Littlefield, 2014.

Fitzgerald, Kathleen J. *Recognizing Race and Ethnicity: Power, Privilege, and Inequality*. Boulder, CO: Westview, 2017.

Gillota, David. *Ethnic Humor in Multiethnic America*. New Brunswick, NJ: Rutgers University Press, 2013.

Hart, Kevin. *I Can't Make This Up: Life Lessons*. New York, NY: 37 INK, 2017.

Kaplan, Arie. *Saturday Night Live: Shaping TV Comedy and American Culture*. Minneapolis, MN: Twenty-First Century Books, 2015.

Kauffman, Susan. *Kevin Hart: Comedian, Actor, Writer, and Producer*. New York, NY: Enslow, 2018.

Kohen, Yael. *We Killed: The Rise of Women in American Comedy*. New York, NY: Picador/Farrar, Straus and Giroux, 2013.

Knoedelseder, William. *I'm Dying Up Here: Heartbreak and High Times in Stand-Up Comedy's Golden Era*. New York, NY: PublicAffairs, 2017.

Lewis, Jenifer. *The Mother of Black Hollywood: A Memoir*. New York, NY: Amistad, 2017.

Littleton, Darryl, and Dick Gregory. *Black Comedians on Black Comedy: How African-Americans Taught Us to Laugh*. New York, NY: Applause Theatre & Cinema Books, 2008.

Luckett, Sharrell D., and Tia M. Shaffer. *Black Acting Methods: Critical Approaches*. London, UK: Routledge, 2017.

Marciniak, Kristin, and Amanda D. Lotz. *Women in Arts and Entertainment*. Minneapolis, MN: Essential Library, 2017.

Mizejewski, Linda, Victoria Sturtevant, and Kathleen Roe. *Hysterical! Women in American Comedy*. Austin, TX: Austin University of Texas Press, 2017.

Noah, Trevor. *Born a Crime: Stories from a South African Childhood*. New York, NY: Spiegel & Grau, 2016.

Peisner, David. *Homey Don't Play That! The Story of In Living Color and the Black Comedy Revolution.* New York, NY: 37 INK, 2019.

Randazzo, Joe. *Funny on Purpose: The Definitive Guide to an Unpredictable Career in Comedy.* San Francisco, CA: Chronicle Books, 2014.

Randolph, Joanne. *African American Musicians & Entertainers.* New York, NY: Enslow Publishing, 2018.

Robinson, Phoebe. *You Can't Touch My Hair: And Other Things I Still Have to Explain.* New York, NY: Plume, 2016.

Toplyn, Joe. *Comedy Writing for Late-Night TV: How to Write Monologue Jokes, Desk Pieces, Sketches, Parodies, Audience Pieces, Remotes, and Other Short-Form Comedy.* Rye, NY: Twenty Lane Media, 2014.

Wassan, Sam. *Improv Nation: How We Made a Great American Art.* Boston, MA: Mariner Books, 2018.

Bibliography

Birnbaum, Debra. "Tiffany Haddish on Pay Parity, Licking Arsenio, and Why Emmys and Oscars Are Overrated." *Variety*. Retrieved October 28, 2018. https://variety.com/2018/tv/news/tiffany -haddish-pay-parity-arsenio-hall-barbra -streisand-1202966627.

Chandler, D. L. "Tiffany Haddish Talks Career, Dating, Upcoming Rap LP & More." *Hip-Hop Wired*, October 19, 2018. https://hiphopwired .com/769393/tiffany-haddish-talks-career-dating -upcoming-rap-lp-more.

Chang, Justin. "Tiffany Haddish Is a Comic Revelation in the Sweet, Sexy and Hilarious 'Girls Trip.'" *Los Angeles Times*, July 20, 2017. https:// www.latimes.com/entertainment/movies/la-et-mn -girls-trip-review-20170720-htmlstory.html.

Chestnov, Alexis. "From Foster Care to *Girls Trip* Star: Tiffany Haddish's Amazing Real-Life Story." *People*, August 27, 2017. https://people.com /movies/from-foster-kid-girls-trip-breakout-star -tiffany-haddishs-life-story.

Gomez, Patrick. "'I Was Basically a 10-Year-Old -Mom': Inside Tiffany Haddish's Inspirational Journey from Foster Care Kid to *Carmichael Show* Star." *People*, April 22, 2016. https:// people.com/tv/the-carmichael-shows-tiffay -haddish-from-foster-care-kid-to-sitcom-star.

Haddish, Tiffany. *The Last Black Unicorn*. New York, NY: Simon & Schuster, 2018.

Hart, Kevin. "Tiffany Haddish." *Time*. Retrieved October 27, 2018. http://time.com/collection /most-influential-people-2018/5217580 /tiffany-haddish.

Kelley, Sonaiya. "Tiffany Haddish Times Three in 'Night School,' 'The Oath' and 'Nobody's Fool.'" *Los Angeles Times*, August 30, 2018. https:// www.latimes.com/entertainment/movies /la-ca-mn-sneaks-tiffany-haddish-20180830 -story.html.

McNary, Dave. "Here's a Quick Guide to All of Tiffany Haddish's Upcoming Movies." *Variety*, August 7, 2018. https://variety.com/2018/film /news/tiffany-haddish-schedule-upcoming -movies-1202897687.

Miller, Liz Shannon. "Tiffany Haddish: Why the 'Girls Trip' Star Is This Year's Comedy Wonder Woman." IndieWire.com, July 19, 2017. https:// www.indiewire.com/2017/07/tiffany-haddish -girls-trip-interview-1201856785.

Orr, Niela. "The Tao of Tiffany Haddish: 'If They're Not Talking about You, Then You're Not Doing Your Job.'" *Glamour*, July 31, 2018. https://www .glamour.com/story/tiffany-haddish-september -2018-cover-story.

Ramos, Dino-Ray. "Tiffany Haddish Talks Being First Female Black Stand-Up Comedian to Host 'SNL',

Dedicates Emmy Dress to Her Family." *Deadline*,
September 18, 2018. http://www.deadline
.com/2018/09/tiffany-haddish-saturday-night
-live-primtime-emmys-creative-arts
-emmys-1202466456.

TV One. "Tiffany Haddish Opens Up About Her
Tumultuous Childhood | Uncensored." YouTube,
February 16, 2018. https://www.youtube.com
/watch?v=bsJlmlkRsLY.

Walsh, Katie. "'Girls Trip' Review: Raunchy but
Heartfelt Female Empowerment." *Chicago
Tribune*, July 19, 2017. https://www
.chicagotribune.com/entertainment/movies
/sc-girls-trip-mov-rev-0719-20170719-story.html.

Index

About the Author

Kevin Hall has written several books for Rosen Publishing, including a few on topics such as YouTube fame and video gaming. Though this is his first book on the subject of comedy, it has been a longtime aspiration to write on this topic.

Photo Credits

Cover, p. 3 Kathy Hutchins/Shutterstock.com; cover background, interior pages (curtain) Kostsov/Shutterstock.com; p. 7 Rich Fury/Getty Images; p. 12 Gabe Ginsberg/WireImage/ Getty Images; p. 14 Splash News/Newscom; p. 15 Alex Millauer/Shutterstock.com; pp. 18, 47 Jeff Kravitz/FilmMagic, Inc/Getty Images; p. 19 Rodrigo Vaz/FilmMagic/Getty Images; p. 21 Fotos International/Archive Photos/Getty Images; pp. 26–27 Steve Grayson/WireImage/Getty Images; p. 28 Michael S. Schwartz/Getty Images; p. 31 connel/Shutterstock.com; p. 34 Jason LaVeris/FilmMagic/Getty Images; p. 37 Andrey_Popov/ Shutterstock.com; p. 41 George Pimentel/WireImage/ Getty Images; p. 49 Michael Loccisano/Getty Images; p. 52 Jamie McCarthy/Getty Images; p. 55 Kevin Mazur/WireImage/ Getty Images; pp. 58–59 ZUMA Press, Inc./Alamy Stock Photo; pp. 62–63 Paras Griffin/Getty Images; p. 66 © AP Images; p. 68 David Livingston/Getty Images; pp. 70–71 Frederick M. Brown/ Getty Images; p. 73 Matt Winkelmeyer/Getty Images; p. 75 Jerritt Clark/Getty Images; p. 79 John Salangsang/Invision/ AP Images; p. 82 Lifestyle pictures/Alamy Stock Photo; p. 86 Dan MacMedan/WireImage/Getty Images.

Design and Layout: Nicole Russo-Duca; Editor: Siyavush Saidian; Photo Researcher: Nicole DiMella